Walter Foster
Jr.

learn to draw

Horses & Ponies

Step-by-step instructions for more than 25 different breeds

ILLUSTRATED BY ROBBIN CUDDY

Inspiring | Educating | Creating | Entertaining

Brimming with creative inspiration, how-to projects, and useful information to enrich your everyday life, Quarto Knows is a favorite destination for those pursuing their interests and passions. Visit our site and dig deeper with our books into your area of interest: Quarto Creates, Quarto Cooks, Quarto Homes, Quarto Lives, Quarto Drives, Quarto Explores, Quarto Gifts, or Quarto Kids.

First Published in 2014 by Walter Foster Jr., an imprint of The Quarto Group.
6 Orchard Road, Suite 100, Lake Forest, CA 92630, USA.
T (949) 380-7510 F (949) 380-7575 www.QuartoKnows.com

Walter Foster Jr. titles are also available at discount for retail, wholesale, promotional, and bulk purchase. For details, contact the Special Sales Manager by email at specialsales@quarto.com or by mail at The Quarto Group, Attn: Special Sales Manager, 401 Second Avenue North, Suite 310, Minneapolis, MN 55401 USA.

ISBN: 978-1-60058-446-6

Printed in China
13

Table of Contents

Tools & Materials

There's more than one way to bring horses to life on paper—you can use crayons, markers, colored pencils, or even paints. Just be sure you have plenty of good "horse colors"— black, brown, gray, white, and yellow.

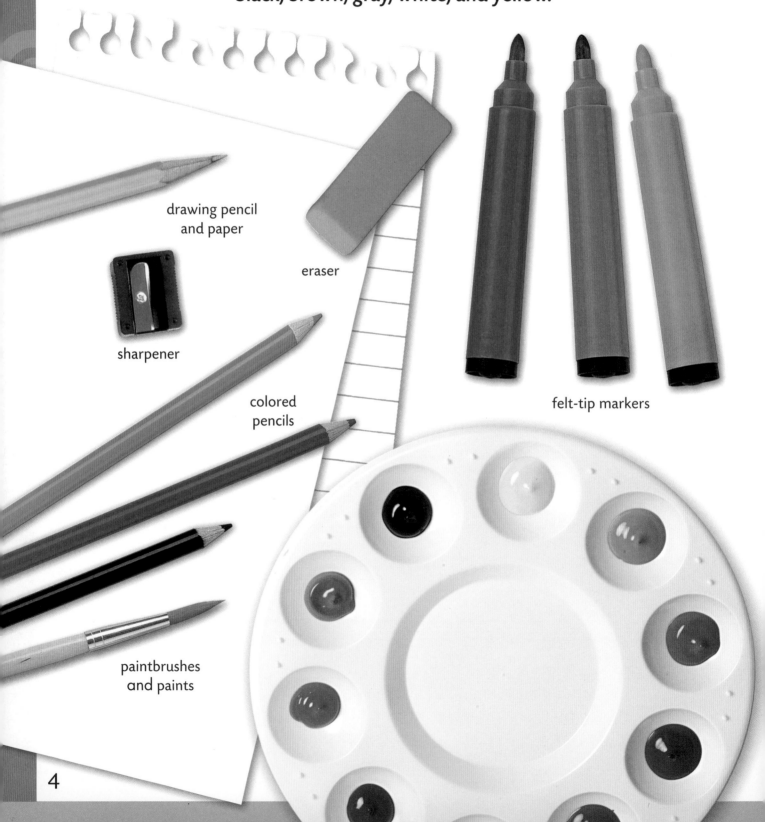

drawing pencil and paper

eraser

sharpener

colored pencils

felt-tip markers

paintbrushes and paints

How to Use This Book

The drawings in this book are made up of basic shapes, such as circles, triangles, and rectangles. Practice drawing the shapes below.

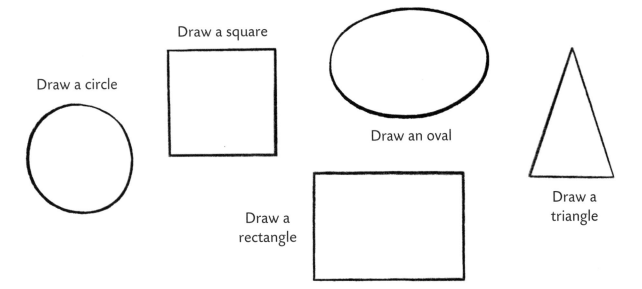

Draw a circle

Draw a square

Draw an oval

Draw a rectangle

Draw a triangle

Notice how these drawings begin with basic shapes.

In this book, you'll learn about the size, origin, and appearance of each featured horse. Look for mini quizzes along the way to learn new and interesting facts!

Look for this symbol, and check your answers on page 64!

Categories

Horse breeds fall into several categories.

Draft Horse

Draft horses are the largest horse breeds and have big, powerful bodies.

Gaited Horse

"Gait" refers to the type or speed of movement. Gaited horses have naturally smooth, comfortable strides.

Light Horse

Light horses are primarily riding horses. They are muscular and agile and have easy gaits.

Pony

Ponies share common ancestry with horses, but they have different body proportions and more primitive features, such as long, thick manes and tails.

Blood Designations

Within horse breeds there are also blood designations.

- **Coldbloods** are draft horses.
- **Hotbloods** are horses with unique bloodlines, such as Arabians, Barbs, and Thoroughbreds.
- **Warmbloods** are light horses, which are a mixture of cold- and hotblood breeds.

Did You Know?

Horses aren't measured in inches or feet like humans. The unit of measurement for a horse is hands. One hand is 4 inches—about the same as the width of a man's hand.

Color Breeds

Some horses are prized for their coat color. These horses can be any breed—only the color is important. In addition to being registered in a breed association, they can also be registered in a separate color-breed association. There are five color breeds:

American White

American Creme

Buckskin

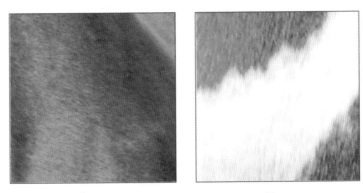

Palomino

Pinto

American Paint Horse

Origin:
United States

Height:
14.2 to 16.2 hands

Color: Bay, black, brown, buckskin, chestnut, cremello, dun, gray, grullo, palomino, perlino, and roan

Type:
Light horse

Blood Type:
Warmblood

Fun Fact!

The American Paint Horse's ancestry can be traced back to the horses of the Spanish explorers who landed in Central America in the 16th century.

The American Paint Horse sports a combination of white and any other color, with markings in all shapes and sizes.

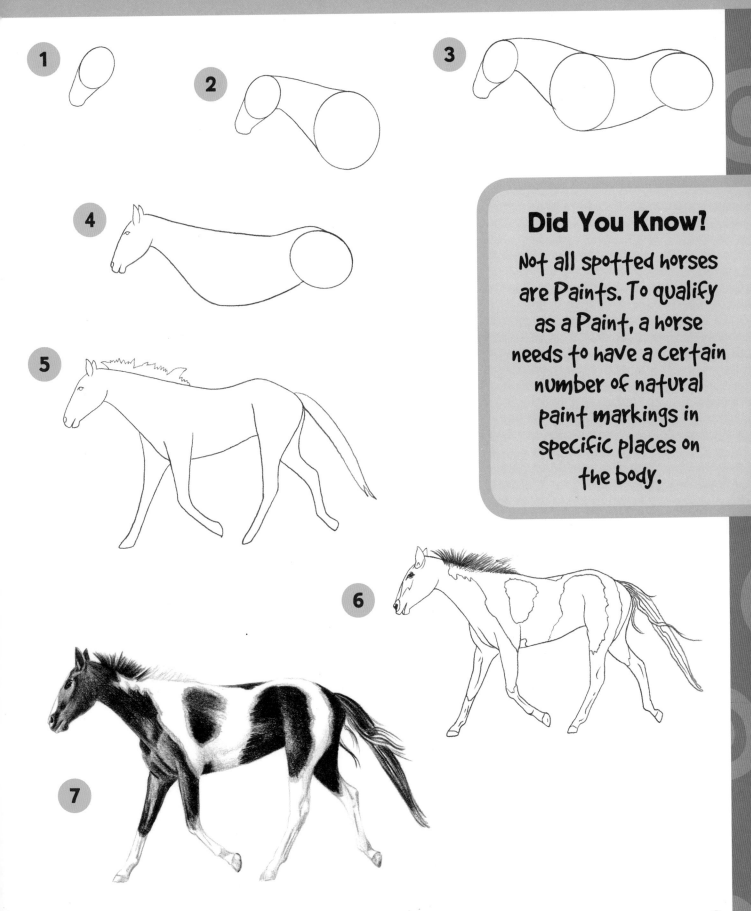

Did You Know?

Not all spotted horses are Paints. To qualify as a Paint, a horse needs to have a certain number of natural paint markings in specific places on the body.

American Quarter Horse

Origin:
United States

Height:
14 to 16 hands

Color: Sorrel, bay, black, brown, buckskin, chestnut, dun, red dun, gray, grullo, palomino, red roan, blue roan, perlino, and cremello

Type:
Light horse

Blood Type:
Warmblood

Fun Fact!

The best American Quarter Horses can run the quarter-mile race—a distance of 440 yards—in 21 seconds or fewer!

The American Quarter Horse is a muscular, compact horse that can run very fast over short distances.

Did You Know?

Quarter horses are a mixture of Arabian-, Spanish-, and English-bred horses.

American Saddlebred

Type: Gaited horse
Origin: United States
Height: 15 to 16 hands
Color: Chestnut, bay, brown, black, gray, roan, palomino, and pinto
Blood Type: Warmblood

Did You Know?

The American Saddlebred is also known as the Kentucky Saddler.

The American Saddlebred has a happy, alert, and curious personality. This horse is the ultimate show horse, known for its high step and elegance.

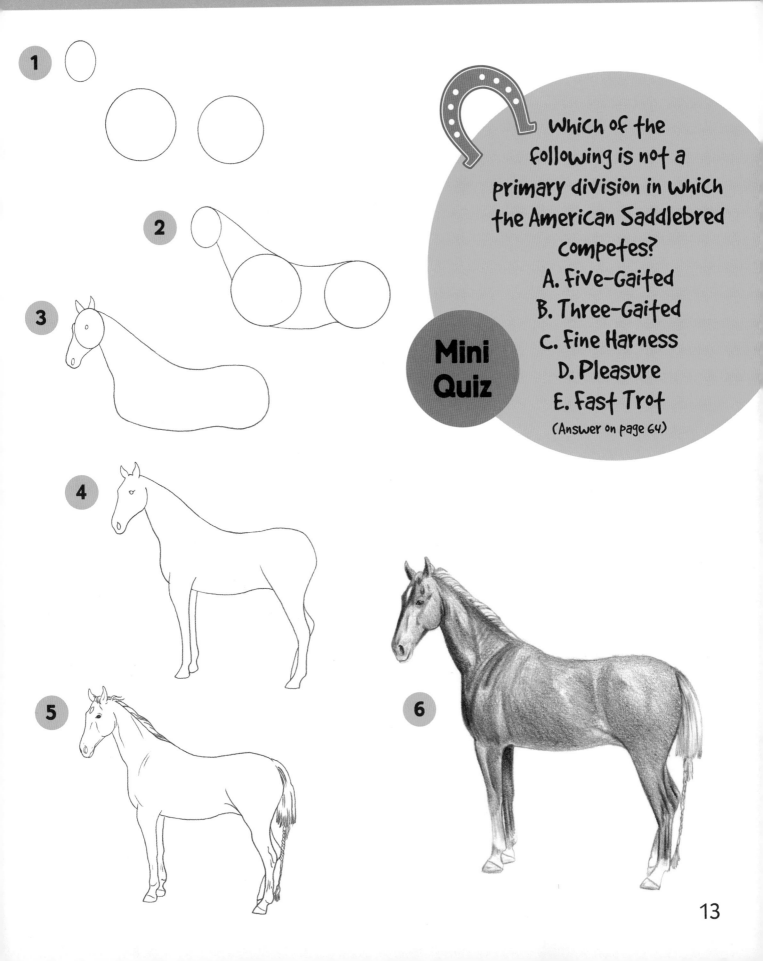

1

2

3

4

5

6

Mini Quiz

Which of the following is not a primary division in which the American Saddlebred competes?
A. Five-Gaited
B. Three-Gaited
C. Fine Harness
D. Pleasure
E. Fast Trot
(Answer on page 64)

Andalusian

Origin:
Spain

Height:
15 to 16.2 hands

Blood Type:
Warmblood

Color: White or gray (sometimes bay, black, chestnut, palomino, or dun)

Type:
Light horse

Fun Fact!

The Andalusian's nickname is "Horse of Kings."

The Andalusian originated in and gained its name from the Spanish province of Andalusia; it is also called *Pura Raza Española* (P.R.E. Horse).

Did You Know?

Andalusians were often used as war horses in ancient combat. The breed is very strong and durable.

Appaloosa

Horse Details

Type: Light horse
Origin: United States
Height: 14.2 to 16 hands
Color: Spotted bay, black, brown, buckskin, chestnut, cremello, dun, gray, grullo, palomino, roan, and white
Blood Type: Warmblood

Did You Know?

The name "Appaloosa" comes from the Palouse River of Idaho and Washington.

Appaloosa horses have a distinct leopard-like print.
This easygoing horse was domesticated by Native Americans.

Mini Quiz

Which state claims the Appaloosa as its state horse?
A. Maine
B. Idaho
C. Florida
D. Wisconsin
E. Texas
(Answer on page 64)

Appaloosa Pony

Horse Details

Type: Pony
Height: 14 hands (maximum)
Color: Spotted bay, black, brown, buckskin, chestnut, cremello, dun, gray, grullo, palomino, roan, and white
Blood Type: Warmblood

Fun Fact!

Appaloosa spotting appears in five patterns: blanket, leopard, snowflake, marble, and frost.

"Appaloosa" is often used to describe distinct spotting patterns on other horse and pony breeds and doesn't always refer to the actual Appaloosa horse breed.

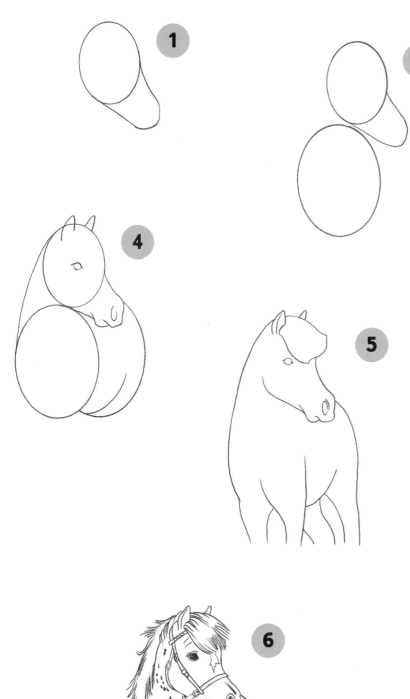

Did You Know?
Spotted ponies often have striped hooves!

Arabian

Horse Details

Type: Light horse
Origin: Arabia
Height: 14.2 to 15.3 hands
Color: Bay, black, chestnut, gray, and roan
Blood Type: Hotblood

Did You Know?

Arabians originated in the harsh desert of the Middle East. As a result, these horses have unparalleled stamina, intelligence, and hardiness.

One of the oldest and purest breeds of light horses, Arabians are relatively small, with protruding eyes, wide nostrils, marked withers, and a short back.

Fun Fact!

The Arabian breed usually only has 23 vertebrae in its back. The typical number for other breeds is 24.

Black Stallion

Children's book author Walter Farley wrote his famous book *The Black Stallion* while he was just a high school student. The book was published in 1941 when Walter was in college.

Did You Know?

Wild horses gather in groups of mares (females) and young foals (babies) and are led by a stallion. When the young male foals reach two years of age, the stallion drives them away. Eventually, the young males gather their own group of mares to lead.

Mini Quiz

What other classic children's story is also about a black horse?

(Answer on page 64)

Clydesdale

Horse Details

Type: Draft horse
Origin: Scotland
Height: 16 to 18 hands
Color: Bay, black, brown, chestnut, gray, roan, and white
Blood Type: Coldblood

Did You Know?

Clydesdale horses weigh about 2,200 pounds on average!

The Clydesdale is a big and powerful draft horse. It has long leg hairs, called feathers, which almost cover its hooves.

1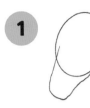

2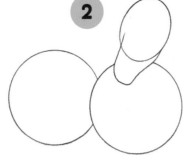

3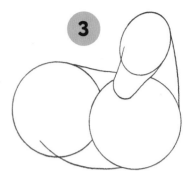

4

5

6

7

Fun Fact!

Although large in size, this breed of horse is gentle and graceful, earning itself the nickname "The Gentle Giant."

Friesian

Horse Details

Type: Light horse
Origin: The Netherlands
Height: 14.3 to 16 hands
Color: Black, brown, and chestnut
Blood Type: Warmblood

Fun Fact!

This breed was developed in Friesland, an island off the coast of the Netherlands, and is thought to have existed as far back as 1000 BC.

Friesian horses, also called Belgian Blacks, have beautiful black coats and thick manes and tails.

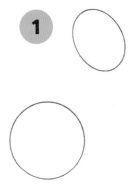

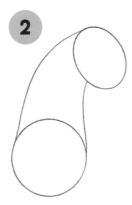

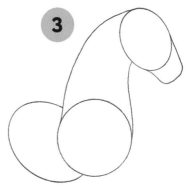

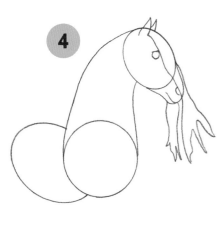

Did You Know?

friesians are talented show horses and excel in dressage, a competition in which horses perform special movements in response to signals from their riders.

Gypsy Vanner

Fun Fact!

Gypsy Vanners—also known as Tinker Horses, Irish Cobs, Colored Cobs, and Drum Horses—are smart and kind, and they love people. They are often used in equine therapy and education programs.

Gypsy Vanner horses have feathering leg hair that starts at the knee and flows down over the hooves. This long hair protects the legs from cold, rain, and snow.

Mini Quiz

True or false: Gypsy Vanner Horses were not bred until after World War II.

(Answer on page 64)

Hanoverian Foal

Origin:
Germany

Height: 15.3 to 17 hands, full-grown

Blood Type: Warmblood

Type: Light horse

Color: Bay, black, brown, chestnut, and gray

Fun Fact!

Hanoverian horse names are traditionally chosen using the first letter of the father horse's name!

A foal is a juvenile horse. The Hanoverian is a popular sport horse breed with a long stride and excellent jumping skills.

Did You Know?

A horse has two sets of teeth during its lifetime. Just like humans lose baby teeth, a foal loses its "milk teeth," and a new permanent set grows in.

Highland Pony

Fun Fact!

The Highland Pony is the largest and strongest breed of all the native ponies in the United Kingdom.

Highland Ponies are strong and sure on their feet. Scottish hunters use them for traveling up and down steep, rocky hillsides and carrying heavy game.

1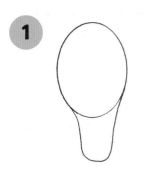

2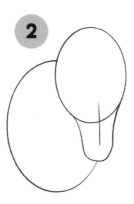

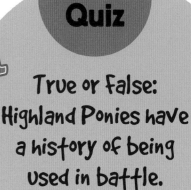

Mini Quiz

True or false: Highland Ponies have a history of being used in battle.

(Answer on page 64)

3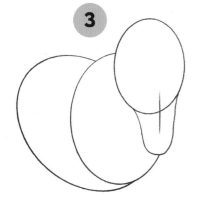

4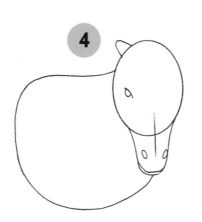

5

6

7

Lusitano

Origin:
Portugal

Height: 15.2 to 16.2 hands

Type:
Light horse

Blood Type:
Warmblood

Color: Bay, black, chestnut, dun, gray, and palomino

Fun Fact!

Until the 1960s, the Lusitano and Andalusian were considered the same breed.

Did You Know?

The Lusitano is named for Lusitania, the name given by the Romans to what is now Portugal.

Lusitanos are athletic and energetic horses and were traditionally used in bullfighting in Portugal.

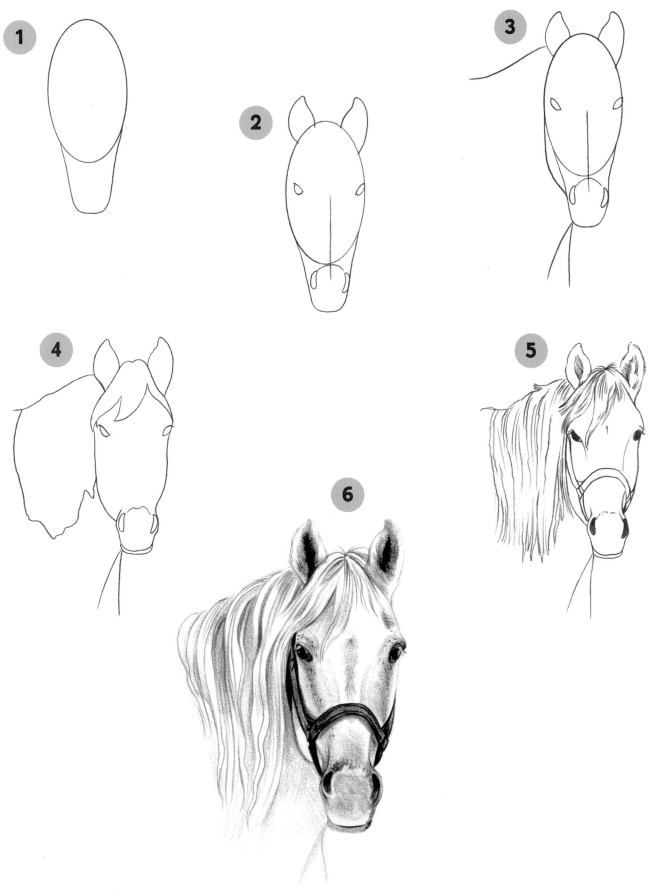

Mare & Foal

Did You Know?

Horses rely on sense of smell to recognize each other. A mare can identify her foal by its smell and find it in a large herd.

Fun Fact!

A young horse is called a foal until it is one year old. When the horse is between one and two, it is called a yearling. Then it is called a colt until it turns four and is considered mature.

Mini Quiz

How soon after birth
can a foal stand up?
A. one week
B. one day
C. Two days
D. Three hours
E. Immediately
(Answer on page 64)

37

Morgan

Horse Details

Type: Light horse
Origin: United States
Height: 14.1 to 15.2 hands
Color: Bay, black, brown, buckskin, chestnut, cremello, dun, gray, palomino, and white
Blood Type: Warmblood

Fun Fact!

This breed is traced back to one horse named Figure in the late 1700s. Figure was given to a schoolteacher named Justin Morgan to pay a debt. As Figure became legendary for his speed in races, he became known as "Justin Morgan's horse."

This athletic and powerful horse is considered to be one of the first native breeds of the United States.

Did You Know?

While the Morgan is not considered a gaited breed, there are some gaited Morgans found within the breed.

Mustang

Origin:
United States

Type:
Light horse

Height:
13 to 16 hands

Blood Type:
Warmblood

Fun Fact!

The word "mustang" is a derivative of the Spanish word mesteña, which means "wild" or "stray."

Color: Bay, black, brown, buckskin, champagne, chestnut, cremello, dun, gray, grullo, palomino, perlino, roan, and white

Mustangs are free-roaming horses that descended from domesticated Spanish horses. They are known for their speed and grace.

Did You Know?

The first Mustangs are thought to have been Iberian breeds, such as the Arabian and Andalusian, brought to Mexico and florida by Spanish settlers.

Norwegian Fjord

Horse Details

Type: Light horse
Origin: Norway
Height: 13.2 to 16.2 hands
Color: Bay, black, chestnut, dun, gray, and palomino
Blood Type: Warmblood

Did You Know?

The Norwegian Fjord is thought to be one of the world's oldest and purest horse breeds.

This small but sturdy breed is often mistaken for a pony. Though small, Norwegian Fjord horses are very strong and hardy.

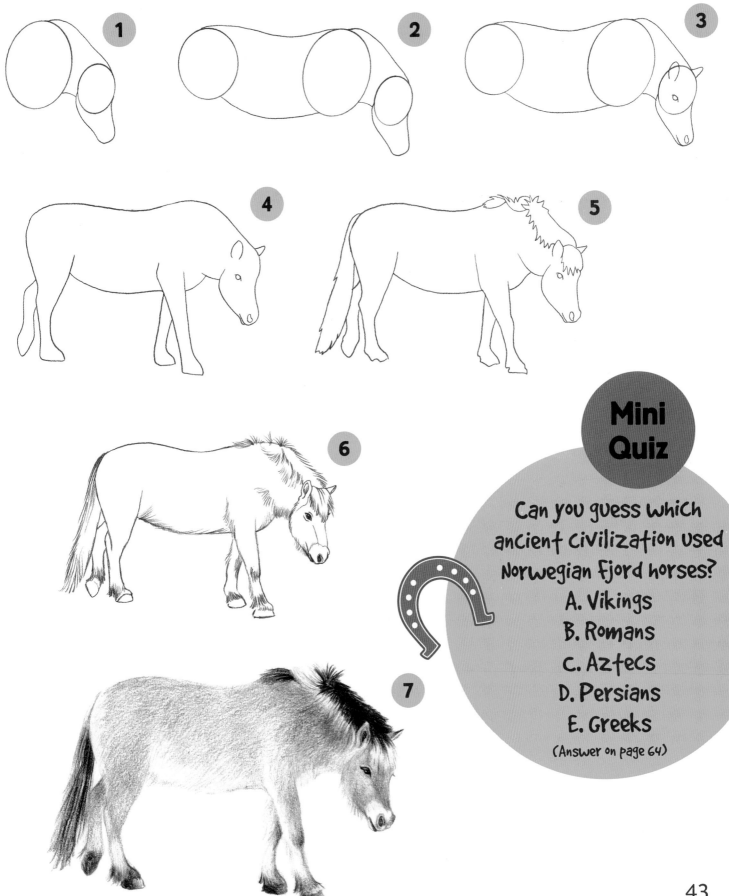

Mini Quiz

Can you guess which ancient civilization used Norwegian Fjord horses?
A. Vikings
B. Romans
C. Aztecs
D. Persians
E. Greeks
(Answer on page 64)

Paso Fino

Height:
13.2 to 15.2 hands

Blood Type:
Warmblood

Type:
Gaited horse

Color: Bay, black,
chestnut, gray,
palomino, and roan

Did You Know?

Paso fino means
"fine step" in
Spanish.

The Paso Fino is an elegant horse with a smooth, ambling gait.
This horse is known for its endurance and being comfortable to ride.

Mini Quiz

True or false:
The Paso Fino walks
and canters, but it
does not trot.
(Answer on page 64)

Percheron

Horse Details

Type: Draft horse
Origin: France
Height: 16.2 to 17.3 hands
Color: Bay, black, chestnut, gray, and roan
Blood Type: Coldblood

Did You Know?

French Percherons are born black and turn gray by age 3. American and British Percherons are gray or black.

This attractive draft horse is an energetic breed that is popular for riding and dressage.

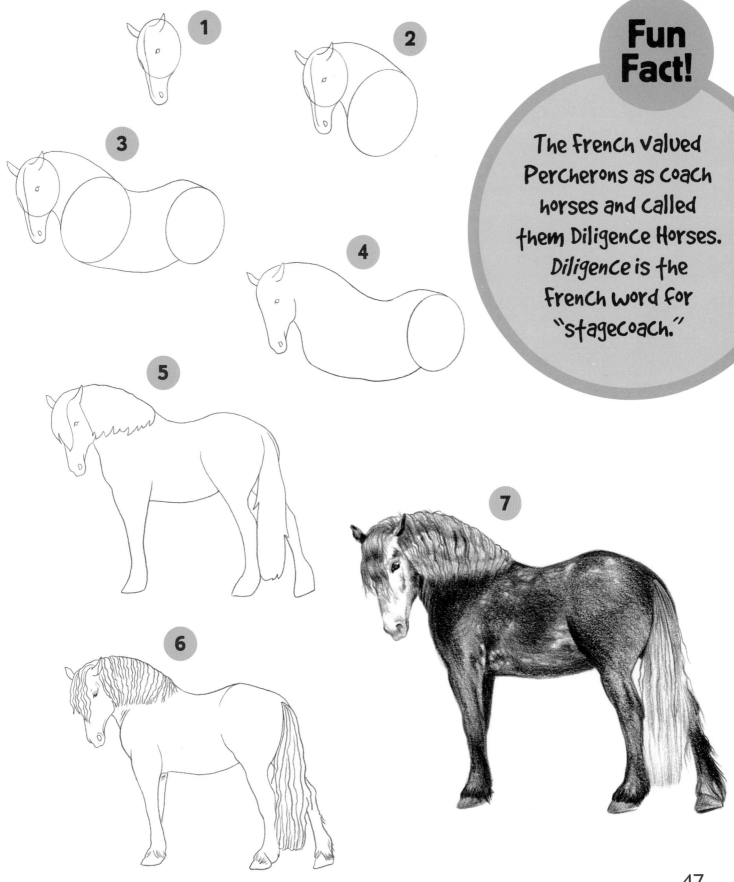

1

2

3

4

5

6

7

Fun Fact!

The french valued Percherons as coach horses and called them Diligence Horses. Diligence is the french word for "stagecoach."

Pinto

Fun Fact!

There are four types of Pintos: Stock, Hunter, Pleasure, and Saddle.

Did You Know?

Pintos and Paints have the same patterns of coloring, but although every Paint is a Pinto, not every Pinto is a Paint.

The Pinto is a color breed and can come from any breed of horse as long as it meets the patterned coat requirements.

1

2

3

4

5

6

Mini Quiz

True or false: Pintos are named after the Spanish word for "painted."

(Answer on page 64)

Pony of the Americas

Type: Pony
Origin: United States
Height: 11.2 to 14 hands

Fun Fact!

It is common for a POA's coat to change with age.

50

This popular breed of pony has a striking appearance and often has similar color markings to the Appaloosa.

1

2

3

4

5

6

Mini Quiz

Can you guess which type of coat pattern is most common for this breed?
A. Blanket
B. Leopard
C. Pinto
D. Roan
E. Tovero
(Answer on page 64)

Shetland Pony

Origin:
Scotland

Type:
Pony

Blood Type:
Warmblood

Height:
9.3 to 11.2 hands

Color: Black, brown, bay, chestnut, and pinto

Fun Fact!

The smallest of the pony breeds, the Shetland Pony is from the Shetland Islands, north of Scotland.

Shetland Ponies may be tiny, but they are very strong and sturdy. This tough pony is strong enough to carry a third of its own weight!

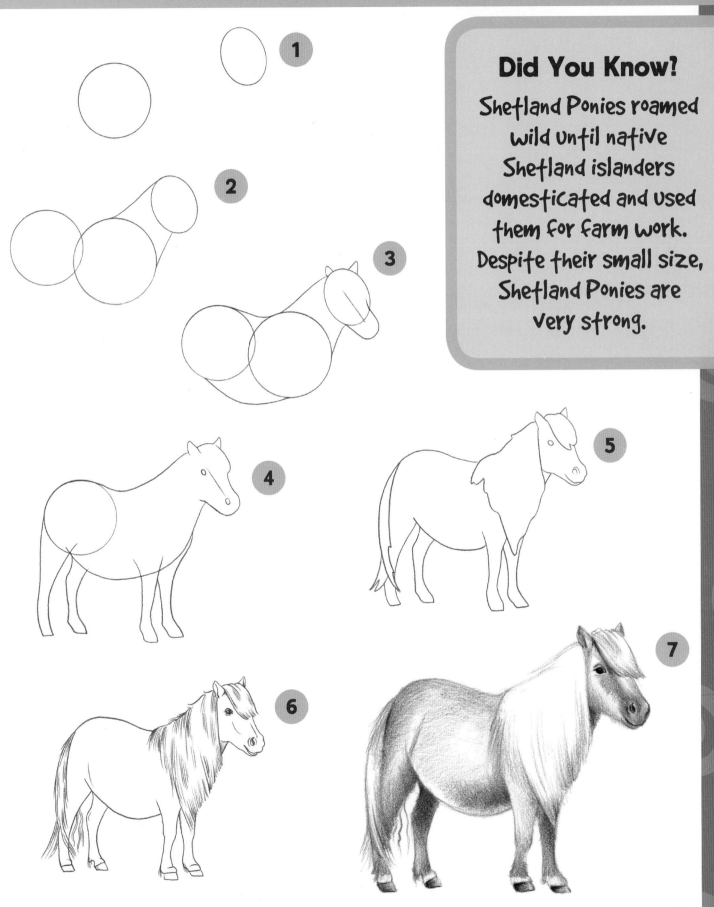

Did You Know?

Shetland Ponies roamed wild until native Shetland islanders domesticated and used them for farm work. Despite their small size, Shetland Ponies are very strong.

Thoroughbred

Horse Details

Type: Light horse
Origin: United Kingdom
Height: 15.3 to 17 hands
Color: Bay, black, brown, buckskin, chestnut, cremello, gray, palomino, perlino, and white
Blood Type: Hotblood

Fun Fact!

This breed was developed during the 17th and 18th centuries in England, and all modern Thoroughbreds descend from three Arabian stallions.

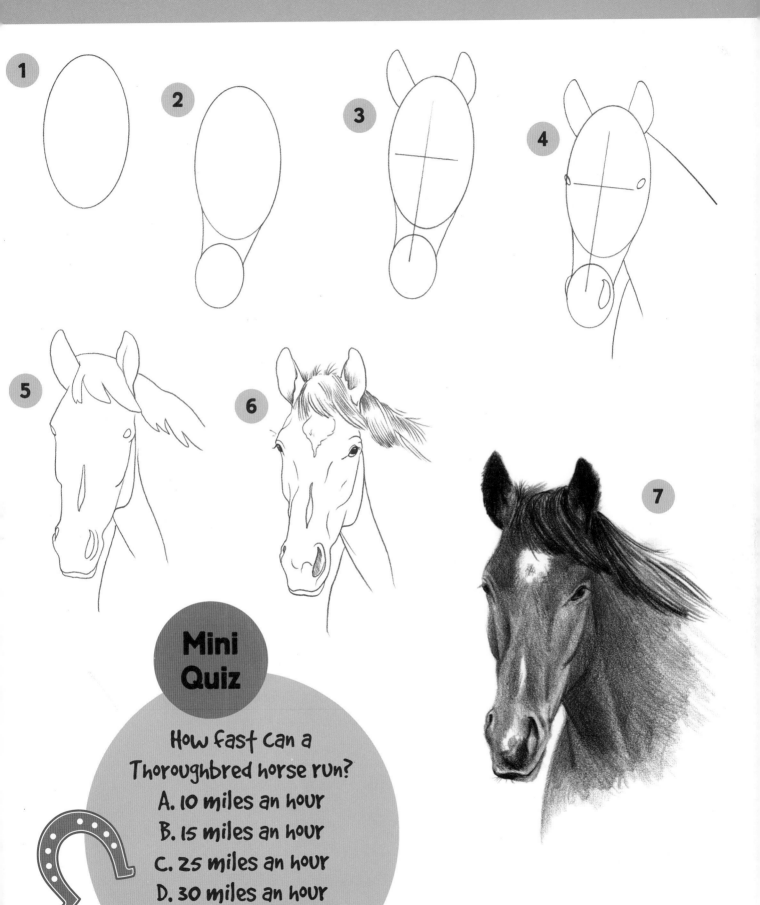

Mini Quiz

How fast can a
Thoroughbred horse run?
A. 10 miles an hour
B. 15 miles an hour
C. 25 miles an hour
D. 30 miles an hour
E. 40 miles an hour
(Answer on page 64)

55

Two Horses Portrait

Fun Fact!

Horses sleep for two to three hours a day, and they sleep longer in the summer than in the winter.

Horses are very social animals and like to live in herds, or groups.

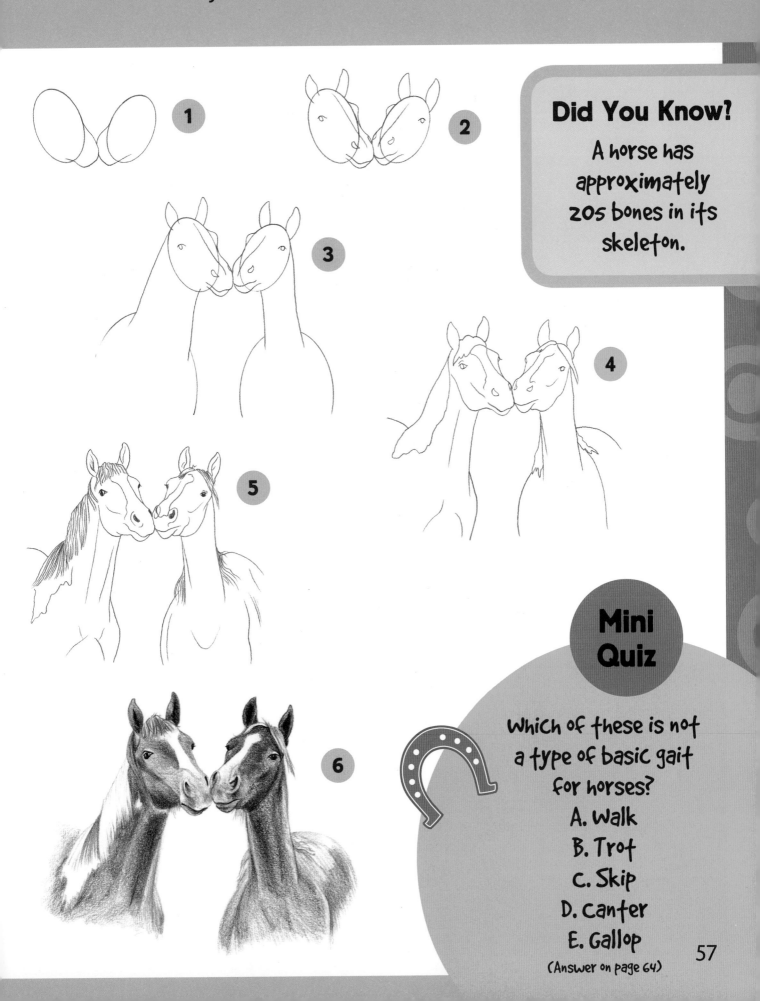

1

2

3

4

5

6

Did You Know?
A horse has approximately 205 bones in its skeleton.

Mini Quiz

Which of these is not a type of basic gait for horses?
A. Walk
B. Trot
C. Skip
D. Canter
E. Gallop

(Answer on page 64)

Two Ponies Portrait

Did You Know?

Ponies live longer than horses. They can live into their 50s, while horses generally live for 25 to 30 years.

Fun Fact! The smallest pony in history, Pumpkin, was only 14 inches tall!

Ponies are more independent than horses, but they are still social and like to be around other horses and ponies.

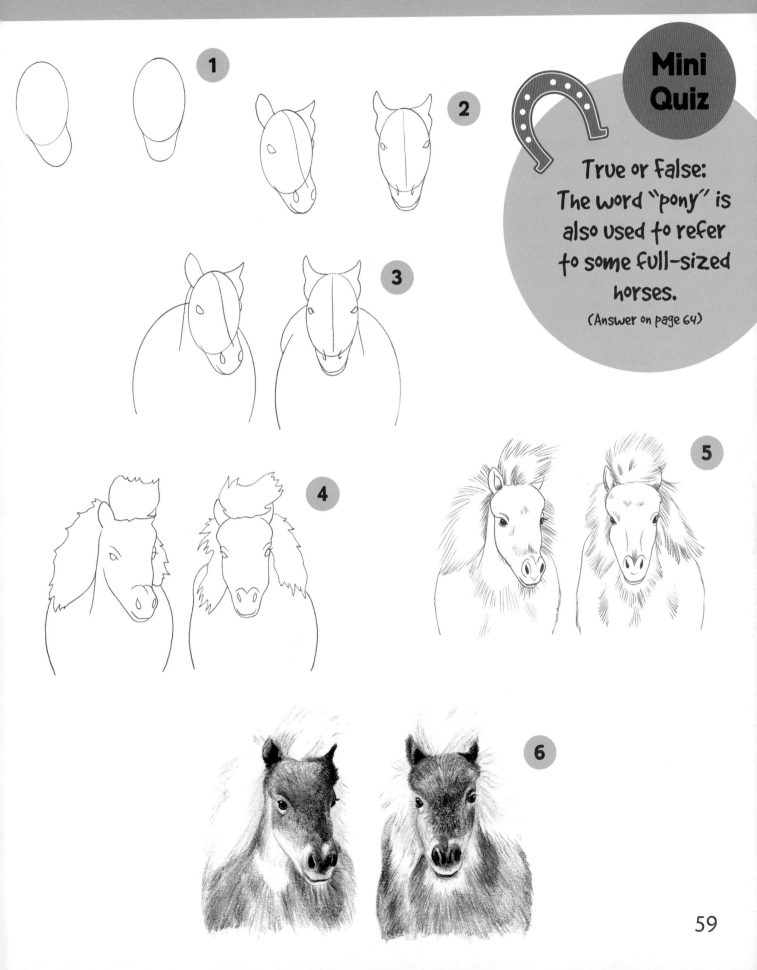

Mini Quiz

True or false: The word "pony" is also used to refer to some full-sized horses.

(Answer on page 64)

1

2

3

4

5

6

Welsh Mountain Pony

Origin:
Wales

Blood Type:
Warmblood

Height:
11 to 12 hands

Type:
Pony

Color:
Any, except pinto

Did You Know?

The Welsh Mountain Pony is the only type of Welsh pony that still lives in the wild in Scotland.

Welsh Mountain Ponies are the smallest of Welsh Pony types. They are hardy and able to survive long, cold winters with very little food and shelter.

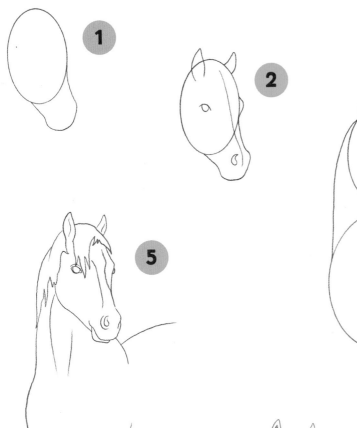

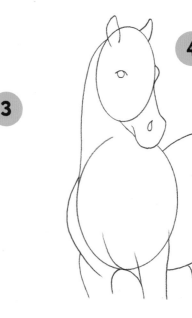

Fun Fact!

The Welsh Mountain Pony was originally used for sheepherding.

Welsh Pony Mare & Foal

Did You Know?
There are more than 200 breeds of ponies!

There are four recognized types of this breed of pony: Welsh Mountain Pony, Welsh Pony, Welsh Pony of Cob, and Welsh Cob.

Fun Fact!

A Welsh Pony mare and foal like to stay very close to each other during the first two months after the foal is born.

Mini Quiz

True or false: Ponies are miniature horses.

(Answer on page 64)

63

Mini Quiz Answers

Page 13: E. Fast Trot. American Saddlebreds compete in the other four divisions, and each division has its own "look," with competitors groomed to perfection.

Page 17: B. The Appaloosa was named the state horse of Idaho in 1975.

Page 23: *Black Beauty*, written by Anna Sewell, was published in 1877.

Page 29: True. After World War II, Gypsy families began breeding horses that would have the endurance and strength of a draft horse and an elegant appearance reflective of Gypsy culture—flashy and magical.

Page 33: True. The Highland Pony was used by warring Scottish clans and was even used in the 20th century during World War II.

Page 37: E. A newborn foal's first instinct is to stand up and eat!

Page 43: A. Vikings. Archaeological records show that Vikings used Norwegian Fjords as early as 2,000 years ago in their explorations and conquests.

Page 45: True. The Paso Fino does not trot. Its natural gaits include the paso fino (slowest), paso corto (moderate), and paso largo (fastest).

Page 49: True. The Spanish word for painted is *pintado*.

Page 51: A. One of the most common patterns for PoAs is blanket, which means the hips and back legs are white. This white hair is usually dotted with spots.

Page 55: E. Thoroughbred horses can run up to 40 miles an hour.

Page 57: C. From slowest to fastest, the basic gaits are: walk, trot, canter, and gallop.

Page 59: True. Some full-sized horses are referred to as ponies, including polo ponies, Indian ponies, and cow ponies. A polo pony is any horse that is used in the game of polo. "Indian pony" and "cow pony" are other names for the American Indian Horse.

Page 63: False. Miniature horses are not the same as ponies. While some miniature horses resemble ponies, these horses are exactly the same as full-sized horses, only smaller. Unlike ponies, they do not have short legs, thick necks, or big bellies.